Legendary Rome

Francesca Brocchetta

CONTENTS

PREFACE

This guide presents the fundamental symbols of Rome in a single itinerary. Through the mysterious enchantment of myths and legends, we'll discover the dawn of the Eternal City and the grandiose Imperial age. From the place where the twins Romulus and Remus were found to the Coliseum, from the Circus Maximus to the shrines of the Forum; Rome's iconic monuments as you've never seen them before

Legendary Rome

Lupercal

The place where the she-wolf suckled Romulus and Remus

Amongst the many tourists walking inside the Circus Maximus or lying along what's left of its stalls, only a few stop to observe a special corner of the Palatine, easily visible from that position. I myself was amazed when I learned that what I had always thought was a legend was becoming history before my very eyes. The most renowned place in the history of Rome, sought after for centuries, seems to have been found. The Lupercal, the place where the she-wolf is said to have suckled the twins Romulus and Remus, has been discovered near the walls of the Augustus' residence, in a hollow below the slopes of the Palatine Hill and in an area never before explored between the Temple of Apollo and the Church of Saint Anastasia. Unfortunately, it's not yet possible to visit this 16-meter deep hypogeum. Nonetheless, archaeologists, using a probe armed with a video camera, were able to capture amazing images of the place. It's a nymphaeum about 9 meters high beneath a vault finely decorated with pumice-stone and seashell mosaics, dominated by a white eagle, symbol of the Emperor Augustus. To the Romans, this place was a sort of shrine where once a year, in February, the miraculous suckling of the twins after they were abandoned to the swollen Tiber was celebrated. The Emperor Augustus wanted to build his second imperial residence right here because it was so symbolic of the history of the city.

The celebrations to honor the finding of the twins were called lupercalia. They were rituals in honor of the god Lupercus, a mythological figure who looked like a wolf and had the function of increasing the fertility of the young women of the Palatine. The festival generally took place like so: the Luperci, young aristocrats identified with the Wolf God had to dress up in goat skins and sacrifice animals, including goats. After offering to Lupercus some bread prepared by the Vestal Virgins (priestesses of the Goddess of the Hearth) with a knife still stained with the blood of the sacrifice, two young men of high birth wet their forehead, and then dried it with wool dipped in goat's milk. Afterwards they cut the goatskins into strips to make whips, and after a rich banquet they probably ran around the Palatine whipping anyone they met. The whip strokes symbolized fertility and increased women's fecundity by helping them give birth. Running around the Palatine was also considered an act of purification. This ritual, which may seem crazy and cruel to our eyes, began to be practiced in ancient Rome following a long period in which the women were barren. Ovid recounts a legend about its origins. A sacred procession of women and men arrived at the sacred wood of Juno, at the foot of the Esquiline Hill, imploring the Goddess to make the women fertile again. The Goddess responded by rustling branches, which was interpreted by an old Etruscan priest: a male goat had to be sacrificed and strips cut from its skin to strike the women's backs; in so doing, each would give birth to a baby after ten lunar months.

Two hills for two twins

Which of the two twins will be king?

Legend has it that, near the banks of the Tiber, in a miserable hovel, lived Faustulus, an old shepherd, with his wife Larentia. One evening Faustulus was sitting by the door of his hovel while Larentia was preparing their evening meal. All of a sudden, they heard a rustle coming from the woods, and there, near the river, a dark shadow slipped down to the bank... Faustulus decided to go and see what was happening. He told his wife to wait for him and he set off cautiously towards the banks of the Tiber. Due to the recent rains, the river had flooded the fields and the ground was covered in large puddles of water. In one of those puddles, at the foot of a tree, Faustulus saw an enormous she-wolf, lying on her side and suckling two babies. Thinking he must be dreaming; he slowly withdrew and went back to the hovel where he told his incredulous wife about the wolf suckling twins; then he took her by the arm and dragged her out towards the river. Shortly afterwards, the two little foundlings were resting in the cozy confines of Faustulus and Larentia's hut, where they grew up, and in a few years became two strong boys, a little wild, but good. Faustulus called them Romulus and Remus. But how and why did the basket arrive at the banks of the Tiber? To answer that question, we must look to mythology. Legend has it that Trojan hero Aeneas, son of the goddess Venus and a mortal man (Anchises), fled from Troy after the Achaeans destroyed his city and established himself in ancient Latium, marrying the daughter of king Latinus (Lavinia) and founding the city of Lavinium. According to the legend, Ascanius, son of Aeneas, later founded Alba Longa and his descendents ruled this ancient Latin city for about two centuries. Many years later, one of these, Numitor, was deposed by his younger brother Amulius who, to avoid any legitimate hairs being born, forced Numitor's daughter, Rhea Silvia, to become a Vestal Virgin. But Rhea Silvia was loved by the god Mars, who took her in a sacred wood where she had gone to fetch water. From that union twin brothers were born. On the orders of their uncle, the mother was condemned to death, as the law demanded for Vestal Virgins who didn't keep their vow of chastity. The river Aniene, where her body was thrown, took pity on her and resuscitated her. King Amulius entrusted the babies to two slaves, with orders to kill them. But the slaves charged with carrying out the order didn't have the courage and abandoned them to the current of the river Tiber. The twins' basket thus landed on the bank near the marsh of Velabrum (a flat area so called in ancient times from the Latin a vehendis ratibus, i.e. "crossable by raft"), between the Palatine, Capitoline and Aventine hills, on the left bank of the Tiber (the area which many tourists visit nowadays to try out with their hands the legend about the Bocca della Verità, unawares that what they're sticking their hands into is nothing more than an old manhole cover from the city's network of sewers). A she-wolf who had come down from the mountains to drink at the river was attracted by the babies' crying, she went up to them and began to suckle them. After numerous ordeals, the twins killed Amulius and returned Alba Longa to Numitor, moving away to found their own new city. Since they were twins and the rules of primogeniture couldn't work as an elective criterion, it was up to the gods who protected those places to indicate, via auguries, which of the two should give his name to the new city and who should reign after its foundation. By tradition, they chose a curious ritual which today we would call "birdwatching". Whoever saw the most birds would be the one chosen by the Gods. So to interpret their signs, Romulus chose the Palatine Hill and Remus the Aventine. The first sighting, six vultures, fell to Remus, it is said. Since Romulus saw twice as many, he was the one who had to take up his plow and plow a furrow (the sulcus primigenius) to mark the boundaries of the city which he called Rome. The furrow had to be plowed anticlockwise according to the ancient Etruscan ritual that dictated that a cow be yoked on the inside and an ox on the outside, the former symbolizing female fertility and centripetal force of the city, the latter the male centrifugal force of the fierce bull that defends the city from outside attacks. The cow and the o also symbolized the deities from which Aeneas and Romulus were descended: Venus and Mars. Venus, fertile on the inside but inviolable virgin on the outside; Mars, warrior on the outside, but propitiatory of wellbeing on the inside. The rule was that nobody, for any reason, could cross the furrow without permission from the boss. But Remus, whether out of jealous or as a joke, jumped over it laughing and said: "Look how easy it is!". Romulus was furious and went for Remus and, with his sword, slew him, exclaiming: "Thus, from now on, whoever dares climb my walls and whoever offends the name of Rome will die." It was April 21st, 753 years before the birth of Jesus Christ. The birth of the new city marked the end of Remus' life.

Romulus, alone, ruled the city wisely. Just like his birth, Romulus' death is also shrouded in legend. He was 54 years old and had been ruling for 33 years when, as he was reviewing his troops on the Campus Martius, a violent storm broke out following a total eclipse of the sun. As soon as the elements calmed and the sun began to shine again, they realized that Romulus had disappeared. It was said that he had been taken up to the heavens by Mars, his father, who had come down in a thick cloud during the storm. Since he had been taken up to heaven, the Romans deified him with the name Quirino. His festival was celebrated on the Quirinal Hill on June 29th. On this same date the two patron saints of Rome, Peter and

Paul, are now celebrated; according to tradition that is the day they were martyred.

The secret name of Rome

Amongst Rome's many mysteries is the mystery of its secret name. The belief that the city had a secret name is based on what has been passed down by many historians. Pliny the Elder, in his Natural History, wrote, "To utter the secret name of Rome outside of the mystery celebrations is considered sacrilege."

The prescription on keeping Rome's hidden name secret was due to fear that an enemy, if he knew it, would have been able to put a curse on the city, revealing its tutelary name by means of a magic spell. The Romans themselves, according to Pliny, when they were about to attack a city, invoked its guardian deity, promising that they would have been more greatly worshipped in exchange for helping the Romans in their enterprise. The evocatio, sanctioned by solemn ceremonies, was a sort of bribe or underhand deal, "do ut des", which had precious little to do with religion or religiousness as we understand the term today. It consisted of fast-talking the guardian deity of the enemy with flattery and promises. An example of this custom is mentioned by Titus Livius when he talks o Camillus who, finding out about the divinity of Veii, invoked her like so: "I beg you, o Queen Juno, who now has a following in Veii, to come victorious with us to Rome where your greatness will have a temple worthy of you." Scipio did the same thing with Carthage, imploring the local gods to desert that place and accept Roman hospitality. Keeping the name of a city shrouded in mystery was a very ancient custom connected with beliefs in the eastern world, which attributed to a name the function of key to magical power. To utter the true name indeed meant to know, to give form to a spiritual image, to reveal the essence of a being, and thus dominate it. Giovanni Lidio, a late Byzantine author, tells us that Rome had three names: the profane and public "Rome", the sacred "Flora" and the arcane and unpronounceable "Amor". This last name is worth looking at more in depth: an ancient graffito of intersecting words which came to light on the wall of a house in Pompeii is rather significant. A magic square made up of words showing the so-called square Rome, in its popular, profane name and also in its sacred name: Roma, the name known to all, and Amor, the name attributed to Venus, a tutelary deity venerated in secret. Indeed, what strikes us the most is that reading the name in two directions represents the deep soul of what Rome has represented during centuries of history. Its double nature evoked at an etymological level: in one direction we have "ROMA" as a mark of strength, valor, and power; read in the opposite direction we have "AMOR", a complement of the millennial history of the city which, from the symbol of conquest and power that it was, has become the capital of spirituality and of the Christian message. Never has there been a truer case of one name, one destiny.

4 The Circus Maximus

Once it was the largest stadium of ancient Rome and not much more than a stretch of level ground covered in grass. Lying between the Palatine and the Aventine hills, the Circus Maximus could hold more than 250,000 spectators. It may seem incredible, but today the world's biggest stadium, the Maracanã in Rio de Janeiro, holds 205,000.

The games and races held there were more than a simple show. Juvenal was the first to understand the importance and influence that these spectacles could have on the masses of the Roman people. He purposely coined the famous saying "Panem et Circenses", a cry of accusation towards the Roman people for have reduced themselves to being content with "bread and circuses", ignoring political affairs and thus leaving the governing classes complete freedom to do what they wanted. Food distribution and public baths and spas on the one hand, gladiators, exotic beasts, chariot races, sports competitions and theater on the other, were none other than a skillful instrument used by the Emperors to placate the masses, and it looks like they succeeded completely. The whole of Rome turned out at the Circus, and the people didn't want to miss the collective folly of the games. Thousands of fans squeezed up against each other gave cries of passion for the young charioteers engaged in mortal maneuvers to conquer the podium.

In the archaic period, the Circus was just as we see it today and the spectators watched the chariot races sitting on the lawn on the hill. It was Julius Caesar who had the first masonry seats built and who gave the building its final form. It was then completed by Augustus who made it a grandiose monument by adding an obelisk from the time of Ramses II, brought over from Egypt. This obelisk was moved in the sixteenth century by the Pope to Piazza del Popolo and is now known as Flaminio. In the year 357, a second obelisk was brought to Rome by order of the emperor Constantius and this too was erected in the middle of the Circus; today it can be found in front of the church of St. John Lateran. The most important races were held during the games in September which had been celebrated since the founding of the city. Initially they were sacred in character and were performed to please the gods, whose statues were taken out of the temples and brought in procession up to the pulvinar, a sacred platform built especially for them.

The chariots racing in the Circus had to do seven laps around the central "spine", a dividing element between the two sides of the track, the outward and inward tracks. Running around the "spine" was a canal, called the euripus, filled with water which the staff could use to cool the red-hot hubs of the chariot wheels. Then, set in a horizontal pole, were seven bronze eggs dedicated to the Dioscuri and seven bronze dolphins. Every time a lap was completed, an egg was turned over and, at the same time, one of the dolphins gave the same indication by dipping its head into an imaginary sea. In a symbolic interpretation, the obelisk of Augustus represented the rays of the sun; the seven laps represented the cycle of time and human life and the eggs alluded to the birth of the universe. Usually the race began with 12 chariots setting off from staggered starting posts, so that the outermost teams were not at a disadvantage. In the single-entry races, on the other hand, each team entered only one chariot. To win, the charioteers had to get as close as possible to the bronze markers, but without touching them to avoid breaking their axles!

The Roman public had a profound knowledge of the qualities of both the men riding the chariots and the horses, and they discussed knowledgeably how the horses should be driven to get the best out of them and to avoid getting wrecked when squeezed on the bends, or how to upset the competition with often risky and unfair maneuvers. Chars and spells to help the preferred faction to win, invocations and magic to provoke falls in other teams were also part of this world. Even the Emperors let themselves get caught up easily in this climate. Caligula had horses and charioteers poisoned to help out the green faction which he supported.

Not far from the Circus you can admire a very original bas-relief, though I'm sure its creator never imagined how famous his work would become in the future. One of his manhole covers, destined for the cloaca massima, Rome's sewer, was set in a wall of the church of Santa Maria in Cosmedin in 1632 and was no longer called a simple manhole cover but instead assumed the mysterious name of Bocca della Verità "the mouth of truth". A great marble mask depicting the head of a faun with holes for the eyes, nose, and mouth. In the Mirabilia Urbis Romae, a medieval guide for pilgrims, the mouth was ascribed with oracular power. In the Middle Ages the legend was developed that Virgil had the Bocca della Verità made to dispel doubts about the faithfulness of husbands and wives. Popular accounts tell of a beautiful young woman, wife of a Roman patrician, who had been accused of adultery because she received visits from another man while her husband was away. When her consort heard about this, he didn't let himself be moved by the tears of the woman, who declared herself to be innocent, but insisted that she be "put to the test" by the Bocca dell Verità. The day the woman had to undergo this test, a young and apparent unknown man came up to her and kissed her. The people present wanted to attack the intruder, but she convinced them to let him go, claiming that he was just a madman. In reality it was all staged because, when the young woman put her hand inside the Mouth, she could proudly claim that she had never kissed anyone apart from her husband and that poor idiot, who in reality was her lover. And so her hand was left intact, much to her husband's satisfaction, but to the extreme humiliation of the Bocca della Verità who felt so dejected at such audacity that from that day on he decided he didn't want to "express" himself any more and no longer closes his mouth to punish   liars.

The other side of the Tiber

It's hard to imagine as you walk through the alleyways on the far side of the Tiber, so full of movement and tourists, that this side of the Tiber, during the early decades after the founding of Rome, was an outside area, impenetrable and dangerous. Here was a place of Etruscan influence and settlements. The Romans feared them because they recognized their supremacy in every field. But who were they and what role did they play in the founding of the city?

Let's begin with a bold claim: the Etruscan soul erected the very pillars of Rome. The rituals, the magic, the aura of mystery which still surrounds this people is worth looking into more deeply. The Etruscans were the most enigmatic and fascinating people who lived in Italy. A famous historian like to say that what we know about them wouldn't fill more than five or six pages in a book. That's dead right. And still today the word most often springs to mind when talking of the Etruscans is "mystery". This term has probably never been used with such conviction and ease for any other ancient people. Some maintain that the Etruscans actually deliberately shroud themselves in mystery, with the precise aim that nothing of theirs ever be known, starting with their origins, and including even the most elementary facts about their existence: their language, their religion, their houses, and the underground streets. This is how the world of the Etruscans appeared to the Romans themselves: an isolated relic of a far-off, lost world, incomprehensible and alien, "neither similar in language, nor similar in customs," as Dionysius of Halicarnasus wrote at the time of Augustus. A long history of contact, relations and exchanges is attested between the two peoples. Rome drew a great many elements which make up its own culture from the Etruscan experience. The meticulous prescriptions on the scrupulous observance of ritual practices was the characteristic that most struck the Romans who had come into contact with this people. To give an example, complex rites followed a lightning strike in a certain place, which was immediately fenced off for precaution and declared sacred. The fulgatores, priests devoted to the study of weather phenomena, with wax in their ears saw off the residual vibrations by chanting a sacred word.

The Etruscan discipline consisted exactly in a meticulous formulary with all the responses to the "heavenly signs" and the relative rites to be carried out when needed. Cicero himself spoke of sacred books which regulated the social and political life of the Etruscans. The sacred text was made up of three books: the Libri Aruspicini, which dealt with divination by interpreting the viscera of animals, the Libri Fulgurales, which contained the doctrine of lightning, and the Libri Rituales, concerning the standards of behavior to follow in public and private life.

The Sacred Area of the Imperial Forums

Roman state religion had very ancient roots and, as in many other cultures, the king of ancient Rome was not only an administrator, but first and foremost a priest, so the religious and political functions came together in him. It is no coincidence that, like the Greek Orpheus, Picus and Faunus, two of the mythical Italic god-kings predating Romulus, also had shaman-like characteristics such as, for example, the ability to speak with the dead. Even in the age of the Republic, religious offices were mostly compatible with political offices. Cicero, for example, was an augur, a priest whose job it was to interpret the will of the gods by watching the flight of birds. Priests, then, constituted a category apart: religious offices were an additional role which citizens could carry out together with their political or administrative job. The emperor had the role of Pontifex Maximus, as he was head of the college of pontifices (priests who presided over religious worship). Furthermore, he celebrated the Suovetaurilia, an ancient rite of purification whose sacrificial victims (hostiae) were a pig, a sheep, and a bull. During the sacrificial ceremony, the meat of the butchered animals was consumed at a banquet, while the bones and fat were burned on the altar. These rites took place at specific times of year, one example is the October equus, a festival which took place during the ides of October. On that date, at the

Campus Martius, there was a chariot race at the end of which the right-hand horse of the winning chariot was killed with a javelin taken from the altar of Mars. The sacrifice represented the closure of the military year and the conservation of the victorious forces, represented by the winning animal.

The Roman calendar was full of festivities, at least one for each month of the year and many Roman houses or inns put up a memorandum next to the door. For example, February takes its name from februare, meaning "to purify", since February was the month of purification; while the first month of the year, January, derives from Janus, the Italic god of beginnings. As the conquests continued, Rome welcomed numerous divinities of vanquished peoples through the evocatio ceremony. The ancient ritual was carried out by Roman priests as they besieged cities. The guardian deities of the enemy city were invoked and asked to abandon their abode and their protégés to move to Rome, where they would receive the highest honors and where a temple and their worship would be immediately consecrated. And so, at the time of its greatest splendor, Rome ended up worshipping around 30 thousand deities! Each one was connected with a different aspect of life, family and public activity. Respect for religion was fundamental, since the rapport with the gods was made up of exchanges, duties, and reciprocal respect, both in public and private rites. Nonetheless, being holier-than-thou was frowned upon, people owed much to the gods, but in the correct doses, since they didn't ask anything more.

The gods manifested their disapproval or their favor through numerous signs in the form of portents mostly from the sky: comets, meteors, the heavenly vault seemingly opening up to let out a bright light, clouds which take on strange forms and seem to come alive, all these were considered Signs. But of all the Signs, the most noble was lightning, because it was sent by the greatest of the gods, Jupiter. His temple, the very heart of the state religion, stood majestically on the Capitoline hill. It was one of the most ancient in Rome, legend attributes is construction to Romulus himself, shortly after founding the city. For the Romans this temple was a symbol of the power and glory of their city; indeed they recount that, when the foundations were dug, a human head came to light, which the diviners interpreted as a prophesy: Rome would one day become the capital of the world (caput mundi). Unfortunately not much remains of the ancient temple today, due both to its demolition in the Christian era and to collapse of this part of the Capitol; nonetheless, part of the remains of the podium is visible within the New Museum of the Capitoline museums. Thanks to archeologists, we can get an idea of its original appearance: it was a grandiose building, with a pillar measuring 2 and a half meters in diameter and gold-plated portals. An imposing structure of over 3000 square meters, considered by many to be impossible for the antiquity of the time. It had 3 cellae, the individual rooms of the deities, since Jupiter shared his residence with Juno, his consort, and Minerva, his daughter. Originally the statue of Jupiter was in terracotta, his face painted red on feast days; that is why, when the emperor rode by on horseback in the triumphal procession to celebrate a military victory, his face was also painted in the same color. In this Temple the consuls offered their first public sacrifices, and here the triumphal processions ended, as well as that all the documents regarding relations between Rome and foreign powers were also kept here.

From the Capitoline hill today the view embraces the entire area of the Forum. The ruins of the marvelous buildings that stood here still hold a great fascination for visitors; but once they would have astounded them! The Roman Forum was the commercial, religious, and political center of the empire's capital, it was rectangular in shape and was connected to the Palatine and the Capitol by the Via Sacra. Between its walls the greatness of Rome and of the nascent Empire was born and developed. Walking amongst these ruins, one can almost hear the echo of the commotion of the victorious procession laden with booty, as testified by the arch of Titus in honor of the emperor who defeated Jerusalem in 70 AD and that of Septimius Severus (from 203 AD) to record the victory over Parthia in present-day western Iran. At the foot of the Capitol we find the temples of Saturn and Vespasian. The temple of Saturn was one of the most venerated in the city, when it was founded Rome was still a farming community. The present remains, a high plinth with eight pillars, go back to 42 AD when the temple was rebuilt. Inside the temple were kept the bronze tablets belonging to the ancient 12 tablets, the collection of laws making up the foundation of Roman law. In the vaults below the stairways and podium was the Aerarium populi Romani also called the Aerarium Saturni the complex of state gold and silver reserves. Saturn was venerated for that faculty of his known as Lua Saturni (in Greek luo means "liberate, untie", and lustrum has the value of "purification"), i.e. the capacity to free the city from disease. For this reason the feet of the statue dedicated to him, a simulacrum in ivory, were tied with woolen cords which were untied only for Saturnalia, during which, every year between the 17th and the 23rd of December, the god was celebrated. On those days social order was overturned: slaves could drink and dine together with their owners and sometimes even be served by them; senators and other high-caste Romans could not wear the aristocratic togas, but donned common clothes; no prisoner could be punished and war could not be declared. The festivities were also celebrated in private houses: gifts such as dolls and wax candles were exchanged and people gambled using walnuts, a symbol of prosperity, as a stake. Much of the spirit and the rituals of those festivals are found nowadays in the Christian Christmas. Opposite the temple of Saturn stands the seat of the Senate, the Curia. This, too, was a temple, since the Senate could only meet on sacred ground. Public assemblies were held in the Comitium, made up of the public square, the curia were the Senate deliberated, and the Rostri (the platform which orators spoke from). One of the most famous speeches given from this platform is without doubt that made famous by Shakespeare in Julius Caesar, spoken by Mark Antony. In this brilliant piece of oratory by which Mark Antony stirred up the Roman plebs against the conspirators who murdered Julius Caesar in 44 BC, he accuses Brutus, who is proud of his own moral integrity and his faithfulness to his friends, of having murdered Caesar by treachery. Here are his words, which play with irony and mockery on Brutus's honor…

"…He was my friend, faithful and just to me: But Brutus says he was ambitious; And Brutus is an honourable man. He hath brought many captives home to Rome Whose ransoms did the general coffers fill: Did this Caesar seem ambitious? When that the poor have cried, Caesar hath wept: Ambition should be made of sterner stuff: Yet Brutus says he was ambitious; And Brutus is an honourable man… "

Continuing our walk we find on the right hand side the temple of Castor and Pollux, all that remains of it are three gracious Corinthian columns. Its story is shrouded in legend. At the beginning of the 5th century BC, Rome, targeted by the nearby Latin cities, decided to make a preemptive attack on them. The clash took place on the banks of lake Regillus around the year 496 BC. During the battle the Romans saw, lined up beside them, two divine horsemen: Castor and Pollux, sons of Leda and Jupiter. The mythological twins then arrive at the city to announce the Roman victory to the people gathered in the Forum. On the spot where this apparition appeared, the son of dictator Postumius, who had led the war against the Latins, had the temple erected. This sacred site, too, is a "safe" protected by the gods; in its foundations is deposited part of the fiscus Caesaris, the imperial state treasure, as well as a precious metal inheritance of some rich Romans who rented what we would now call a strongroom. At the end of the square on the Forum stands the candid temple of Vesta, goddess of the hearth and sister of Juno and Ceres (the goddess of the harvest, from whom the word "cereal" derives). Today only a few white pillars remain to remind us of the temple's former splendor.

Inside there were no statues, just a sacred flame symbolizing the eternity of Rome. The priestesses of the virgin Vesta, custodian of fire, were chosen from amongst Roman girls aged between 6 and 10 years, belonging to noble families; they had special privileges but had to keep their vow of chastity. They lived in the house of the vestals, a sort of convent made up of a courtyard enclosed within colonnades along all four sides, with a fountain and pool at the center; on the baths the statues of the most important vestals can still be seen. The best preserved specimens have been transferred to the Museo Nazionale Romano. The task of the priestesses was to keep the sacred fire burning, not as simple a task as it might seem, since a gust of wind would have been enough to blow out the flame. If the fire were to go out, it would bode ill for Rome, but more so for he Vestals, because it would mean that one of them had committed impure acts. The incriminated vestal was buried alive, since it was sacrilege to spill her blood, and her lover was flogged to death. The fire had to be relit in the most difficult way, by rubbing sticks together. Apart from this harsh rule, the Vestals could benefit from numerous privileges, they enjoyed immense financial resources and high prestige. Their social relations were so highly thought of that they were entrusted with looking after wills, treaties and other important documents and treasures. Their priestly service lasted 30 years, after which they were freed from their vows and could even get married. But there was widespread belief that the jealous gods drasticall shortened the lives of their husbands, and so many of them remained in the temple, unmarried, even after their discharge.

Our next stop is the Temple of Antoninus and

Faustina, going back to the mid 2nd century AD. A marble building sitting on a high pedestal with a brick stairway in front, at the center of which the remains of the ancient altar are still visible. Dedicated to the emperor Antoninus Pius and his wife Faustina, it was transformed into a church in the Middle Ages since it was thought that on that spot Saint Lawrence had been condemned to death. The pillars of this temple have resisted every attempt to knock them down and at their tops can still be seen the deep scars left by workmen's cables as they tried to topple them. The buildings present in the Forum stayed up, creaking but largely intact, up until the 16th century. Then many were demolished by the Christians who salvaged material to build churches and especially for the new Vatican.

Before we arrive at the Coliseum we'll stop for a moment at the majestic Temple of Venus and Roma. Venus, goddess of love and beauty, who surpassed all of the other deities in charm and gracefulness, had a very important role in imperial worship. She was the ancestor divinity of the Roman people and especially of the Julius-Claudia family, as she was the mother of Aeneas, as Virgil tells us in the Aeneid. Her temple was built in 135 AD by the emperor Hadrian who drew up the plans and wanted it with two cellae in which the two divinities would be worshipped. The goddess Roma was the personification of the city of Rome, so loved and admired by the ancient Romans that they worshipped her as a goddess. She was depicted armed with a spear and helmet and holding a sphere which represented perfection of form, completeness and balance. Hadrian's political intent in uniting the figure of Venus, mother of Aeneas, with the city of Rome, was to create a continuity between the divine origin of the Julia family and the Roman empire. Of the grandiose temple today, there remains the great cell facing the Coliseum, dedicated to Venus and that facing the Forum, dedicated to Roma. The latter, half engulfed by the convent of the church of Saint Frances of Rome, is a gem restituted to the world by recent restoration works. It is hard not to be enchanted by the monumental pillars of porphyry and the finely decorated marble floor.

The Tomb of Romulus

Amongst the many tourists visiting the Roman Forum today few stop before the slabs of black stone, near the Curia. Yet here, and especially in the vault, down a few steps, is the compendium of many pages, some shrouded in mystery and others laden with magic, from the most ancient period of the city. This is the place which is traditionally called Lapis Niger which in Latin means "Black Stone".

In this precise spot Romulus, the founder of Rome, was murdered by some senators because of his despotic rule or, according to another legend, was taken up into heaven after being struck by lightning, a sign of sacredness and of being chosen, since lightning is sent by Jupiter. By going down a few steps below the current ground level, we arrive at what is left of one of ancient Rome's most important monuments.

To us it looks like an ancient U-shaped altar with an austere plinth in the shape of a truncated cone next to it which must have been the base of an imposing statue, now vanished. A little behind that a funerary stele bears an inscription with one of the most ancient written specimens of the Latin language ever found, the first in public use. It is a religious prescription, perhaps a ban on passing through that place, on pain of being condemned to the gods of hell: "Whosoever violates this place ba cursed," it says.

In the republican era, the whole area above the Lapis Niger was fenced off and covered by a black marble floor from which it takes its name. This was perhaps because the place had taken of dark connotations due to the profanation of the burial which took place during the sacking of Rome by the Gauls in 390 BC.

The Coliseum

Do we really know this monument, symbol of Rome? Even just reading the legend, we discover that its real is not Coliseum, but the Flavian Amphitheater, so called because it was built by Vespasian, the first emperor of the Flavian dynasty. So why did everyone start calling it the Coliseum in the High Middle Ages?

We have to imagine that in the area where we can admire it today there was the Domus Aurea complex, the grand residence Nero had built for himself after the fire in 64 AD. At the precise spot where the imposing monument now stands there was an enormous artificial lake annexed to the villa and called Stagnus Neronis. It was 6 meters deep and contained an enormous quantity of water, indeed it took four days to fill it. In the great portico in front of the villa stood the Colossus: a bronze statue more than 35 meters high depicting Nero with attributes of the Sun God, with a globe in his hand and a crown formed from seven rays, each one six meters long. An imposing presence, the biggest bronze statue ever made, which gave its name to the entire area roundabout, marking its destiny.

This arena of great dimensions could accommodate not only gladiatorial combat, Munera, but also Venationes, a sort of wild animal hunt. At 50 meters high and 527 meters in circumference, the amphitheater was an unforgettable testimony to the greatness of Rome. Each level of its characteristic travertine arcades is of a different architectural order: the first is Doric, the second Ionic, and the third Corinthian. The next level up was made from cement reinforced with bricks, and the top level, the attic (a name which has survived to indicate the very top floor of a building), was in wood, with poles on it to fly flags. In the upper cornice thick shelves served as a base for the poles holding up the linen Velarium or awning which covered the amphitheater, protecting spectators from sun and rain. The task of opening the Velarium was entrusted to an attachment of sailors from the fleet of Cape Misenum, who were particularly adept at performing the complicated operations necessary. Around the Coliseum were (and are still partly visible) big blocks of travertine which served to anchor the cords necessary for the ingenious maneuvers. Since the arena held tens of thousands of spectators, there were no le than 80 entrances, each one marked by a number above the arch (76 for ordinary spectators, two reserved for the imperial family and its entourage, and two for gladiators). Inside, the corridors were so wide, the system of ramps and passages so efficient, that the amphitheater could be filled up in less than 20 minutes; at the end of the show the spectators emptied out onto the streets so rapidly that the corridors were nicknamed vomitoria.

The shows took place on the 3000-square-meter

arena, which was covered with wooden boards and sand, necessary to soak up the blood spilled during combat. Below was a dense network of tunnels necessary to house the scene equipment and the elevators used to keep and move the wild animals. What we se today inside the Coliseum are these tunnels. The cavea, whose bleachers could seat more than 50,000 spectators, had at each side of the shorter axis the platform of honor reserved for the emperor and high-ranking people; the other spectators sat on the bleachers according to a hierarchical order based on social rank, with the most modest section of the population relegated to the upper ring of the building where they watched the shows standing up.

Despite the multitude of spectators crowding the bleachers, from almost every angle the arena seemed surprisingly close, this was due to its elliptical shape which let the spectators get close to the action. The amphitheater also provided one of the few chances to see the emperor in the flesh: it was there that he interacted with the people and from this exchange we can learn much about the state of affairs in Rome at that time. Carefully dosed, the spectators were an effective vehicle of popular consent and confirmation of power. Popularity was the best guarantee of security for an Emperor, and so sovereigns competed to offer ever more grandiose and exciting shows.

For the hunting and fighting between animals, one could see a forest, artfully prepared, emerge from the arena floor, animals appeared as if by magic: lions, panthers, and elephants were only a few of the exotic animals put on show to testify to the vastness of Roman conquests. On one occasion there was even a display of trained seals, to the great joy of the public who obviously knew absolutely nothing of the existence of such animals. More frequent, however, were human combatants who had to deal with the most ferocious beasts from all over the Mediterranean basin. The frenzy for the arena had caused the extinction of entire species in some regions, and it is estimated that at least a million animals died in the arena. The public's favorite shows were the gladiatorial combats. When they entered, the doors beneath the triumphal arch burst open dramatically, the crowd began to whisper, to clap, almost as if to call their darlings, while at the edge of the arena some small "orchestras" played a triumphal march. The entrance procession was made up of two lectors who held up the banner of the organizer of the games for that day. Following them were players with long horns and a cart with a big sign outlining the program of events, the equivalent of a mobile billboard. Afterwards came the slaves carrying helmets and swords, the gladiators' tools. And finally came the true stars of the moment: the gladiators. We can imagine the crowd delirious as they make their entry, and for a moment we feel that even the Coliseum could crumble under the clamor of the crowd as they explode into a unanimous shout, a sudden thunder amplified by the amphitheater itself which acts as a sound box sending echoes throughout the city. A roar of habet ("he has got one!") let's us know that a man has been struck, while a shout of peractum est ("he's finished!") indicated a lethal blow. A gladiator who was no longer able to fight held up his index finger, asking for mercy not from his adversay but from the editor, i.e. whoever had organized the games. Naturally he acted according to the Emperor's indications, who in turn generally followed the opinion of the crowd. A popular gladiator who had fought well received a shout of mitte ("let him go!"), while for others the crowd might chant Iu-gula! Iu-gula! ("Kill! Kill!"). If death was chosen the crowd fell silent. A gladiator had to die courageously. The defeated combatant bowed his head, kneeled down and grasped the thigh of his adversary-turned-slayer to hold himself steady. The executioner plunged his sword from the head into the neck vertebrae of his victim, down the heart. Once killed, the gladiator was dragged away through the scary gate of the dead, the Porta libitinensis, to then be stripped of his armor, which was returned to his fellows. The winner received prize money for the combat and a palm leaf symbolizing victory; in some cases even a gold crown.

It sends a shiver down your spine to think that the four and a half centuries of activity in the Coliseum make it the bloodiest place on Earth. Neither Hiroshima nor Nagasaki produced such a concentration of death. In the limited space of the arena hundreds of thousands of people were killed, according to some even more than a million! As an irony of fate, the Coliseum is today the monument used as a symbol in support of the international campaign against the death penalty. Since 2000, every time a death sentence is commuted to another punishment, annulled or abolished, in any part of the world, the internal lighting of the monument participates in the event by changing the color of the light from white to gold.

ABOUT THE AUTHOR

Francesca Brocchetta. After earning a degree in Humanities at the "University of Rome La Sapienza", she worked for different government departments dealing with land development, culture and tourism. For several years she has worked with digital magazines as a contributor and has been the editorial director of the weekly online journal Paritànews whose focus is equal opportunities, labor, and immigration rights. She is the author of many travel guides dedicated to her authentic passion: the art and culture of Rome.